INDIE AUTHOR CONFIDENTIAL

SECRETS NO ONE WILL TELL YOU ABOUT WRITING

M.L. RONN

ABOUT THIS SERIES

.

This isn't your typical writing self-help book. This series is a compilation of lessons learned from an indie author trying to walk the path to success. Follow author M.L. Ronn (Michael La Ronn) as he navigates what it means to master the craft of writing, marketing, and running a profitable publishing business. Learn from his successes and failures, and learn about things that most successful authors only talk about behind the scenes.

To read all the collected volumes of this series in an anthology, visit www.authorlevelup.com/confidential.

CONTENTS

BECOME A TECHNOLOGY-DRIVEN WRITER

BECOME A DATA-DRIVEN WRITER

BECOME THE WRITER OF THE FUTURE

IDEAS YOU CAN STEAL

INTRODUCTION

This book is a gamble.

I'm not writing to market.

I'm not writing about the usual things you'd expect to see in a book for writers.

Instead, this book is a captain's log of sorts with lessons I've recently learned on my writing journey.

This book idea came to me in March 2020, during the dark, early days of the COVID-19 pandemic, when I was trying to focus my energy on productive activities rather than reading the news.

I recommitted to learning and improving in all areas of my writing life while the world was shut down. Every week, I wrote down lessons I learned about writing, marketing, and more. I decided to turn those learnings into an ongoing book series.

I'm a big believer in the concept of "evolving publicly." I don't hold myself out as a guru. I've built my nonfiction writing business model on sharing information with the community as I learn it. In many ways, I'm "documenting" my writer's journey, as Gary Vaynerchuk often suggests.

Today, writers don't document their progress until they're

successful. One of the bestselling books for writers of all time, *On Writing* by Stephen King, wasn't written until he was already a household name. This is true of virtually every book for writers written by a mega-successful author.

It would be ludicrous for an unknown writer who isn't making a living from their work to write a book about becoming a successful writer, right? Right?

Yet that's exactly what I'm doing.

Success is the result of many decisions and advantages that pile onto each other. New writers who want to walk the path of successful writers can't see all those decisions. All they can see are the big, most recent ones. They don't see the failures, bad decisions, bad luck, or important revelations that led to success.

Maybe by writing this series, I can uncover more clues about what it takes to be successful and share those with the community.

Instead of waiting to write the *one* book about success, I'm writing my first one now, and I'm publishing often.

Like I said, this book is a gamble. It's contrary to how we typically do things in our community.

I also recognize that it may seem presumptuous for a (largely) unknown writer to claim they're going to be successful. I may be an unknown, but I've accomplished a lot so far: I've written over 50 books of science fiction and fantasy and self-help for writers, I host a YouTube channel for writers with over 25,000 subscribers and counting, and I managed to build a writing career while raising a family, working a job at a Fortune 100 insurance company, and attending law school classes in the evenings. So I'm not a complete newbie with unrealistic expectations; I'm working hard toward a successful writing career, and I hope this book will reflect that.

My hope is that you'll find ideas and lessons in this book that you'll never find anywhere else. You won't hear other influencers in the community talking about this stuff publicly. It's not marketable, and it's probably not what their communities want.

I tend to live on the fringe, and I'm comfortable there. If you are looking for more basic writing advice, you won't find it in this series. Check out my other books for writers instead. But if you want something different, unusual, entertaining, and perhaps a little controversial, keep reading.

How This Book is Organized

As a writer, my mission is to create content that entertains and/or educates my audience, preferably both. I do this by focusing on five strategic priorities:

1. Become a world-class content creator
2. Become a world-class marketer
3. Become a technology-driven writer
4. Become a data-driven writer
5. Become the writer of the future

I believe these five priorities are most important for me to have a long-term sustainable career.

I need to master the craft of writing and content creation, which will take the entirety of my lifetime. I'm not in a hurry, but I have a quiet urgency to learn as much as I can quickly.

I need to keep finding ways to sharpen my marketing. Every author must learn to do this.

I need to harness technology to make my writing business more efficient. In a world where technology is rapidly evolving, writers also have to keep evolving. The biggest advantage we have in the market is that we can be nimble. How can we embrace streamlining, automation, and outsourcing so that we can remain nimble no matter how the sands of the industry shift?

I need to harness data to make better decisions that will keep my business profitable. Data is all around us, but how can we capture it and make it more useful? Authors and data don't always mix, but in our rapidly evolving future, data will become ever more important. In fact, I suggest that we'll need to start thinking of our books as data, just like we learned to think of them as products.

And finally, I need to become the writer of the future. The indie writer in 2040 is going to look drastically different than he or she looks today. How will they be different, why will they be different, what trends do we need to pay attention to, and what do we need to do to position ourselves today so that we can thrive tomorrow?

This Book Came from a Wake-Up Call

For me, the pandemic was a wake-up call to start thinking about the future.

Traditional publishers found themselves in dire straits because of their business model. Indie authors experienced record sales numbers because the pandemic favored *their* business model. The comparison between traditional and self-publishing could not have been more contradictory, but that contrast got me thinking...every industry sector experiences a fall at some point. Indies aren't invincible.

My revelation was that I can't continue to do the same things I'm doing today and expect to still be growing in 2030 or even 2040. As great as the increased sales feel, I don't want to wake up one day in the future and be in the same situation traditional publishers are right now—facing the extinction of my business because I failed to adapt and take advantage of trends and emerging technology.

I'm leaning into the discomfort of change even though I don't have to.

I'm giving you a fair warning that sometimes I venture down paths that don't immediately make sense. At times, you may think "Huh?" That's okay.

On the Meyers-Briggs Test, I am the rarest of personality types: INTJ, which stands for Intellection, Intuition, Thinking, and Judgmental. My spirit animal is an octopus, which describes me perfectly if you've ever read any of my books or met me in person.

On the Clifton Strengths Assessment, my five strengths are Strategic (Thinker), Intellection, Futuristic, Achiever, and (wait for it) Learner.

Because of my personality type, I tend to think long-term, and I connect dots that don't seem connectable. For a long time, I thought there was something wrong with me because most people don't think this way. I've learned that it makes me unique. The more you double down on your strengths, the more successful you will be, so that's exactly what I'm doing with this book.

What's in This Volume

From deep dives into mega bestseller fiction techniques to sneaky copywriting tricks to the power of databases, this volume is wide-ranging.

The contents reflect my soul-searching to find the best path forward for my author business during the panic of the pandemic.

This book is organized by my strategic priorities, with about

12 lessons in each section. The chapters are concise and to the point so you can absorb the lessons quickly.

The *Ideas You Can Steal* section contains ideas that I think could be game-changers if the right people took them on. I invite you to dream with me in this section.

And lastly, I have included links to the content I created during the time I wrote this book. I'd love it if you checked it out.

As a final note, this book assumes that you have basic knowledge of certain concepts such as ebook aggregators, metadata, artificial intelligence, and cryptocurrencies, to name a few. I do my best to explain most of them at a high level, but if you need a primer on all the basic industry terms that indie writers need to know, consider reading my book, The Indie Writer's Encyclopedia. It'll help you grasp any concepts I don't cover in-depth in this book.

Thanks for reading this very experimental book. My sincerest hope is that it helps you in some way.

M.L. Ronn
Des Moines, Iowa
July 15, 2020

BECOME A WORLD-CLASS CONTENT CREATOR

BECOME A VIRTUAL APPRENTICE

In a pandemic world, it's hard to keep a mentorship going. You can't exactly meet your mentor for coffee.

Most people are too busy and too stressed out in a pandemic, so why not develop a virtual apprenticeship instead?

Pick a mentor you admire that has a strong Internet presence. Study every single thing that person has written or done and take copious notes.

Learn one or two things per week. You'll be amazed at what you've learned by the end of the year.

I've done this for years with fiction writing. I have studied mega bestsellers for the last few years, and I have learned a lot from practicing their techniques.

This year, I started doing the same thing with marketing and copyright, after hearing some advice from Dean Wesley Smith. I want to improve my marketing and my knowledge of copyright.

For marketing, I started with Seth Godin. I already read his blog every day, but there's much more I can learn. I consumed as many of his blog posts and videos as I could, and I read a few of his books.

For copyright, I took a copyright law class in my final year of law school. The other students weren't interested in the topic and just wanted the credit; I was the most engaged student in the class because copyright law was the main reason I went to law school. Each week was really just a conversation between me and the professor because no one else participated. I came with a lot of questions and was always the first to volunteer to dissect cases. I got a first-class copyright education from a practicing copyright attorney without having to pay legal fees.

With my marketing and copyright "masters," I pretended that I knew nothing and absorbed everything they taught me. I tried new ways of thinking and new ways of approaching my business as a writer.

For example, Seth Godin published a blog post about "bridges and tunnels." Bridges are monuments that stand the test of time and are revered by the public. Tunnels are invisible because they are underground, and not as glorious. However, tunnels are more important because they signify progress. How much better are all of our lives because of sewers, subway systems, and other infrastructure that lay beneath the surface of our busy society? The lesson in Seth's 100-word blog post was that you need both bridges and tunnels as an entrepreneur. Your bridges will attract attention, but it's your tunnels that will truly advance you in life. That got me thinking about what my bridges and tunnels were as an authorpreneur. I decided at that moment that I needed to stop building bridges during the pandemic and focus on tunnels—the world was too anxious to admire any bridges. If I focused on my business and improved my invisible infrastructure, I could emerge from the pandemic and build even bigger and more beautiful bridges. That got me thinking about ways to be more efficient, which led me to my book sales database project, which was my banner accomplishment for the year. All of that happened because of a 100-word blog post that I read in the mindset of a virtual apprentice.

When you study someone for as long as I did, you start to intuitively know how they will respond to questions you have. When you have a question, you can use the virtual mentor in your head. When I read copyright cases now (something I do once a week), I imagine what my professor would think about the cases, and the Socratic questions he would ask.

Virtual apprenticeships are a great tool, and in my opinion, a secret weapon.

IRAC—A UNIQUE WAY OF LEARNING CRAFT

I fell behind with my law school classwork and found myself studying all day. From sunrise to sunset one Saturday, I dissected twenty cases.

When I finished studying, I should have gone to bed, but I did some chores and listened to an audiobook—I think it was one of *The Dresden Files* audiobooks. I heard a chapter that captivated me, and I wondered how the author did it.

Then my mind immediately tackled the problem the same way I would tackle a law school case, which led me to a new way of thinking about the writing craft.

In law school, when studying cases, lawyers are trained to use the IRAC method, which stands for Issue, Relevant Law, Analysis, and Conclusion.

The first element in any case you must understand is the issue at hand. Court justices usually state the issue at the beginning of the case, but not always. Lawyers are trained to spot issues quickly. An example of an issue would be "To what extent should an employer respond when an employee faces death threats and harassment at the workplace?" or "Is an advertisement copyrighted?"

The second element you must understand is the relevant law and why it is at issue. In other words, what is the law that both sides are arguing over?

The third element you must understand is the analysis. How did the court analyze the issue and relevant law, and what is their reasoning?

The fourth element is the conclusion, also known as the holding, which is the decision the court made.

Law school students learn the IRAC method because you have to answer law school questions in the format. They internalize it and carry it with them throughout their lives.

What if you could apply IRAC to fiction writing as a way to dissect how an author wrote a passage of fiction? What if it could help you improve your craft?

I brainstormed the idea and came up with an IRAC of my own: Issue, Relevant Books, Analysis, and Conclusion.

Let's say that you read a scene where a beloved character dies at the hands of the villain. It's a sad scene, but it enthralled you and you want to know how the author did it so you can do something similar in your novel.

First, what is the issue? Who is the character, what level of importance do they have, how do they die, and when do they die? In this case, the issue might be "How do I kill a supporting character at the hands of a villain at the end of a novel?"

Note the specificity. It's a supporting character, not a main character. The character dies by the villain, not by disease or bad luck. And the character dies at the end of the novel, not in the prologue or in the middle. But for this problem, we're focused on a narrow issue: how to kill a supporting character at the hands of a villain at the end of the novel.

Next, in what books can you observe this issue at work? Start with the current book you're reading, but there may be other books you've read in the past or will read in the future that use the same technique.

Next, analyze the passage and break it into a series of steps. Think of it like a recipe. Then do the same thing for other relevant books and compare the recipes. The commonalities are the essential ingredients for replicating the scene in your fiction. But do note the differences between the books because those can give you clues on how to stylize your implementation of the technique. Maybe Book 1's dying character is a best friend, but Book 2's character is a love interest. If your character is a family member, their death is going to elicit a different response that would be somewhere between the death of a friend and a lover.

Finally, take the commonalities that you find and write them down as your conclusions. Then, as you keep reading more books in the future and see additional character deaths, you can update your conclusions.

Follow this method and you'll become a pro at spotting issues in fiction right away. It worked wonders for me.

I developed this method for studying mega bestsellers' work. If I could learn from the top authors in the world, I could improve my craft exponentially.

Anyway, this was a major breakthrough for me and I produced a series of fiction craft videos on YouTube that delve into issues like how to write minor characters, fight scenes, and more. You can view it at www.authorlevelup.com/irac.

HOW TO WRITE MINOR CHARACTERS

I received a question from a YouTube subscriber requesting for me to do an IRAC deep-dive into a specific craft issue. She had a lot of minor characters in her novel and felt like she was "collecting people."

The issues were: how many minor characters is too many, and to what extent do I need to develop each minor character in a story?

In discussing the issue with the subscriber, we discovered that she was talking about walk-on characters, not minor characters. A walk-on character is a character who serves a singular purpose but doesn't do very much in the story other than help it move forward in some way.

In reviewing a few relevant books by mega bestsellers, I learned some important lessons.

To answer the issues, there is no limit to the number of walk-on characters you can put in your novel. Every writer is different and each story has its own demands.

With developing walk-on characters, I learned the following lessons:

- 5 out of 6 of the walk-on characters had names.
- Each walk-on character had an obvious, singular purpose in the story.
- Almost every walk-on character had NO physical description. Instead, the author used a smart character tag (such as an attorney carrying a briefcase). The authors left the rest to the readers' imagination and were careful not to contradict any images the reader formed in their heads.
- The more you visualize a character, the more the reader thinks they are important.
- Visualization equals importance, but dialogue and action do not. So while readers ascribe importance to a character depending on the level you describe them, you can have a walk-on character talk and perform as much action on the page, and readers won't ascribe those as importance. This means that the best way to convey walk-on characters is through dialogue and action.
- In the books I reviewed, each walk-on character appeared three to four times on average.
- All the walk-on characters I studied received zero character development.

These observations were based on studying the walk-on characters in three books, but they were helpful to understand.

You can watch this video as part of my IRAC playlist on YouTube at www.authorlevelup.com/irac.

EXTERNAL LINK VALIDATION IN CALIBRE

I've often said that Calibre is one of the most underrated ebook tools on the Internet. The app started as a way for readers to easily side load books onto their e-readers, but it's also a stellar ebook formatting tool for people who need a free solution.

Calibre has an external link validation tool that will check all of the links in your book to make sure they are valid. I first discovered it several years ago; I didn't have a need for it at the time, but I took a mental note.

When I was finalizing my book *150 Self-Publishing Questions Answered*, I had a large resources section with many external links. I had double-checked the links, but I wanted extra peace of mind since I was writing the book for The Alliance of Independent Authors (ALLi). Since ALLi is a nonprofit, I wanted to make sure the book left a good impression on readers.

I used Calibre's external link checker, and sure enough, it found two broken links that I had missed.

I published the book with confidence that all the links were valid, which will result in a more positive reader experience.

LESS FLEXIBILITY REQUIRES MORE CREATIVITY

After I used the external link validation tool in Calibre, I realized that even though all the links in my book were valid today, they might not be valid a year from now.

Since the book was being published by ALLi, I knew I would have less flexibility in making updates.

Instead of putting my resources section at the back of the book like I originally planned, I removed it from the book and put it on an unlisted webpage on ALLi's website. This way, we could easily make changes to the resources without having to republish the book. This would also help the book remain ever-green. Ultimately, it's an extra step for the reader, but a better long-term experience for them.

SPRINKLE IN THE QUIRKY

I was reading a book about a technical topic that honestly could have been bland and boring: Microsoft Excel's Power Query. But the author had such a great writing style and he used practical examples that were so helpful that I couldn't stop reading. I consumed all of his books in an afternoon.

One of the ways he reeled me in was with his first chapter. He talked about where he was born, where he's lived and worked—you know, all the usual stuff. And then he talked about how he made a ghost pepper peanut butter cookie that won a bunch of awards, and how he likes to tell stories at storytelling events on the weekends. Those two little details were so interesting and quirky that I wanted to keep reading. I wanted to get to know the guy, even though he was talking about a dreadful topic. I ended up reaching out to him and we struck up a great friendship.

Sprinkling in interesting details about yourself when you get a chance is a great idea. It's also a great idea to do this with characters. Wouldn't your readers be intrigued if your protagonist said they created an award-winning ghost pepper peanut butter cookie?

WRITING WITH THE AUDIOBOOK IN MIND

I have produced around 15 audiobooks, so I know a lot about what it takes to create one.

But it wasn't until I narrated my own audiobook that I truly understood what I was doing wrong.

Writing for ebook and print is easy—we do it without even thinking. But there are unique things you have to keep in mind when writing for audio.

I like to use bulleted lists in my nonfiction books. I like how clean they look on the page. However, they are shockingly difficult to narrate. I feel bad for the poor narrators that had to navigate them in my early nonfiction books.

I discovered a few key tips to write books that translate better into audio: shorter sentences, fewer commas per sentence, no bulleted lists, and no parenthetical asides unless they are at the end of a sentence. Each of these elements serve as speed bumps that make it hard to narrate effectively, which translates to a poorer experience for audiobook listeners. Learning to adjust my writing style will be a big adjustment for me, but it will make a big difference in listeners' enjoyment of my audiobooks.

A SIMPLE AUDIOBOOK NARRATION TRICK

In recording my first audiobook, I accidentally narrated the first few chapters too fast.

I spoke too quickly and had no idea I was doing it. I tested my audio while mowing the lawn and I couldn't keep up with my voice.

I imagined what a fast-talking audiobook might sound like to a listener—probably not good. People listen to books while they're commuting, doing chores, taking their dog on a walk, or exercising. They need time to hear and process the message.

When I re-recorded those chapters at a slower pace, I was surprised at how much longer they were; a 30-minute chapter lengthened into 42 minutes.

Multiply those results by the entire book, and you get 12 minutes by 15 chapters, which is 180 minutes, or 3 hours! All because I narrated the book *correctly*.

A comfortable pace is easier to listen to, and therefore more accessible. Longer audiobooks command higher prices, which means more profit.

MY #1 FAIL FOR THE YEAR

I took a gamble in recording the audiobook version for *150 Self-Publishing Questions Answered*. The book had just been copy-edited, so I felt confident that the proofread wouldn't result in too many errors that needed to be re-recorded in the audiobook version.

Since this was my first audiobook, I needed to know if my equipment worked and if I could pull it off. I was eager to start recording, and the proofreader was taking longer than expected.

I took a risk and recorded the audiobook version before the proofreader was finished.

Huge mistake.

I had to rerecord nearly 75 sentences, which was an administrative nightmare. It was, without a doubt, my most expensive mistake of the year. It took approximately eight hours to fix everything. I didn't get much sleep that week, and I was extra cranky.

To put the eight hours in perspective, I can write 2,000 words per hour toward a novel. I lost 16,000 words, or 22% of a potential novel.

Very expensive mistake.

PROFESSIONAL INDEXERS: A NOBLE PROFESSION

Did you know that there is such a thing as a professional indexer?

Their sole job is to create indexes and glossaries for ebooks and print. There's even an American Society for Indexing, with other similar organizations around the world.

According to their website, their membership is open to "all interested persons: professional indexers, editors, publishers, librarians, and anyone else curious about indexing."

You can find indexers on websites like Upwork, or even with a simple Google search.

Indexing is a noble profession that will one day be lost to artificial intelligence, and future generations of writers will never know it existed. Yet it's so intriguing.

I discovered the professional indexer profession as I was producing my book *150 Self-Publishing Questions Answered* with The Alliance of Independent Authors (ALLi). ALLi is a non-profit organization for self-published writers with a mission of ethics and excellence in self-publishing, and they hired me as their Outreach Manager. The book, a joint effort between me and ALLi, is written in a question-and-answer style and addresses the most common self-publishing questions. ALLi has a blog with over 2,000 helpful articles, a podcast network of over 200 episodes, and a YouTube channel with hundreds of self-publishing advice videos. The organization sits on a figurative goldmine of advice, so I pitched a book that tapped into and organized the wealth in that mine. The goal was for the book to serve as a value to their members as well as drive new membership and revenue to the organization. (If you're not a member, join ALLi today at www.authorlevelup.com/alli. We'd love to have you.)

Because of the book's unique nature, I suggested to ALLi that an index could be useful for readers who want to use the book as a resource in the future. Fortunately, ALLi was already in the process of putting indexes in their existing books for writers.

I thought we could find someone to do an unremarkable index in Microsoft Word. Little did I know that my suggestion would open the door to a new galaxy for me. The indexer created a "glindex," which is a hybrid between a glossary and an index. Who knew?

The indexer not only did a great job, she incorporated the index into my Vellum file, which amazed me because I don't have to go through her if I want to make future edits to the book. The "glindex" took the book from good to great because it improved its intrinsic value.

I will be including "glindexes" in all of my writing books moving forward where it makes sense. Though there is a cost, it's a simple way for me to improve the value and utility of my books so that they serve as a helpful resource even after readers finish reading. Plus, almost no one in the indie space is doing it.

AUTHENTICITY MATTERS

During the George Floyd protests and racial unrest here in the United States, I decided to break one of my main rules.

I NEVER talk about race, politics, religion, or current events. I am not in the business of polarizing people. I accept everyone in my community regardless of who they are or where they come from...except if they spew hate, of course.

I decided to make a video and share my story of how racism has affected me. I kept it short and to the point, but I got pretty vulnerable. You can view it at www.authorlevelup.com/racism.

I was afraid the video would be taken poorly. I was also afraid that I would have been misunderstood or maligned for talking about my blackness.

Instead, the video was one of the best performing videos on my channel. Many of my black subscribers commented that they had the same experiences and felt validated. Non-black subscribers appreciated hearing the story. I received a flood of fan mail.

Yes, there were trolls. A few dozen people disliked the video and probably unsubscribed.

Two people told me to go back to Africa, and three people

acted as if a race problem didn't exist in the United States; I banned those people immediately from my channel. Eliminating them makes my community a better, safer, and more inclusive place.

I learned that sometimes it's okay to break your own rules and let your guard down.

UPDATING OLD CONTENT

In 2014, I did a video showcasing the writing gear and equipment I use. It wasn't a popular video, but it did drive decent affiliate income. For example, I sold a lot of Blue Yeti USB microphones from that video, which netted me nice sales commissions.

In 2018, I did an updated video to showcase my new gear since I had made some updates over the years. It drove more affiliate income.

As my YouTube channel grows, I plan to start doing these types of videos annually because they're easy to do, and equipment questions are some of the most common fan mail questions I receive.

BECOME A WORLD-CLASS
MARKETER

HOLDING OUT VS. GETTING IT OUT

This isn't a marketing lesson per se, but it is.

When you're working on anything, you have two choices.

You can work on it until it is good enough, and then release it.

Or, you can work on it until it is better than good enough, and then release it.

With "good enough," you're trusting in your creative process.

With "better than good enough," it's usually perfectionism.

But there are times when "better than good enough" is your only option.

This year, I began recording my own audiobooks. Fortunately, I have a prior career in music with a lot of exposure to audio engineering, so it was easy for me to get started.

However, I quickly ran into trouble with getting my voice to sound like what you hear in professional audiobooks. That said, the audio quality was still serviceable, and I could have easily put it on the market.

But the sound quality didn't meet my personal standards. I decided it was best to spend money and get some help. After working with an audio engineer, we got my audio to sound clean and smooth, almost like what I imagined in my head. Now I know exactly how to replicate this sound in the future without having to hire an engineer. While the audio wasn't celebrity audiobook narrator quality, it was good enough that I felt comfortable releasing it.

I didn't allow myself to fall into the trap of perfectionism—the process of getting help took two days. If I didn't hold out for those two days, I would have let myself and readers down. My audiobook wouldn't have been nearly as good.

So, while I never recommend perfectionism, there is a time and a place for holding out. You just have to have the courage to know when to draw the line and push your product into the world.

EASY REPURPOSING

When I was promoting my book *150 Self-Publishing Questions Answered*, I had the opportunity to do a guest blog post on ALLi's' blog. But it didn't make sense to write a 1000-word blog post about how I wrote the book. I didn't think people would be interested. I felt it was better to lead with value.

I asked if it would be okay to make the blog post an excerpt from the book. I copied and pasted 1000 words from the book, with a short introduction and call-to-action at the end of the post that promoted the book with buy links.

Additionally, I included the audiobook sample that aligned with the excerpt so readers could listen if they chose. Since the audiobook is not exclusive to Audible, I can do whatever I want. It was a simple but effective way to promote the audiobook.

Overall, creating the content took about 15 minutes, which was a win.

SURVEYING MY AUDIENCE

I came up with an amazing idea. I found a way to auto-calculate your book sales without any data entry, and I found a way to create a book sales database that houses all of your sales reports at the click of the button so that you analyze them to your heart's desire.

I thought authors would love it, so I did a 12-week-long blog series chronicling my adventures in building the database and I even did a three-part YouTube series on the idea.

I asked my audience to take a survey about how they track their book income, and out of my entire 20,000 to 30,000 member audience, only six people took the survey.

Six people.

No one was interested enough in the topic to even click on the survey link.

Even though I built the database for myself (and it was a game-changer for me), I decided that it was something the majority of my audience wasn't interested in. I also blame the pandemic; people were distracted and focused on other things.

I proceeded with the project anyway because I believed it

was important, but surveying my audience gave me realistic expectations about how a book sales database product might perform with my community.

ADVANCE REVIEW COPY TRICK

When promoting my book *150 Self-Publishing Questions Answered*, I started promoting the ARCs about a month before I sent them out. I talked about it on my podcasts and YouTube channel.

I used Book Funnel's Certified Mail feature, which was very, very cool because it automated the entire process. The open rates on the emails Book Funnel sent were above-average too.

I also sent readers a link to the audiobook M P3s, even though the audiobook wasn't published yet. It's a nice value-add I haven't seen anyone else do.

COPYWRITING TRICK

When email marketing, short sentences keep readers moving down the page.

One to two sentences per paragraph is all you need.

If you start with a compelling subject line and hook, readers won't be able to resist scrolling.

Putting a simple call-to-action at the bottom of the email makes it even better, preferably inside a button.

Arial size 16 or 18 is the perfect font that has worked wonders for me.

Almost no photos is better because it keeps the focus on your copy.

Anyway, if you've gotten to the bottom of this, be sure to join my email Fan Club and you can see the copywriting lessons I've learned in action.

THREE-STEP SALES METHOD

I read a book called *New Sales Simplified* by Mike Weinberg. I bought it because I accepted the role of Outreach Manager at ALLi. My job was to reach out to companies with services for authors to entice them to join ALLi as Partner Members. It's a sales-driven role, and I've never been in a true sales job. In fact, I've never thought of myself as a salesman. I wanted to read a book that could mentor me before starting the role.

The core message in *New Sales Simplified* is that sales is three steps:

1. Pick a target
2. Employ weapons
3. Develop a plan of attack

Battle symbology aside, the book offers some interesting perspectives of what it means to be a salesperson. It offered many fun thought experiments and gave me ways to stretch myself into a skill set that always made me uncomfortable.

I needed to pick a list of organizations to target. In my case, I focused on organizations for writers. There are a lot of writer's organizations, but most of them cater to traditionally-published writers. Many of them recognize the rise of indie authors but don't know how to help members that have indie aspirations. If ALLi could build inroads with those groups, it could be a win-win.

By focusing primarily on writing groups, I could learn their "language" and get better at selling ALLi's services to them, even if I failed in my first few prospects.

I'm still too new to rate myself in the Outreach Manager role, but the three-step sales tip was helpful in shifting my mindset.

BE A BAT

A flock of bats lives near my house. They circle my roof occasionally, and they freak my dog out.

Bats are nearly blind and can't see well. They use echolocation to get information about their surroundings. They send out sound waves, and those waves reflect off surfaces and back to the bat, giving it a perception of its surroundings—a tree branch, predator, or its next meal.

Creating and marketing products is like echolocation. You send things into the world, like sound waves, not knowing whether they will ever return.

Think about how many sound waves a bat sends out that never come back. The same is true with marketing our books. Some marketing tactics work; others fail and we almost never know why.

When we do receive a signal—sometimes it's an unexpected win. It could be an audience we never considered, or a new marketing platform, or something as simple as a reader comparing your book to a well-known book you've never heard of before.

It's almost always worth paying attention to every signal because following them allows us to fly more confidently, even when we can't see.

USING MY ASSETS

I have more communication channels than your average writer: a YouTube channel, three podcasts, a (not frequently updated) blog, multiple mailing lists, and three websites. I need to do a better job of utilizing them to promote my work.

I was watching YouTube and observed two different mega influencers use subtle video editing tricks to promote their books. They displayed a banner ad at the bottom of the screen with the book and a URL. While it only showed for a few seconds, it was a smart and unobtrusive way to advertise the book. This got me thinking about additional ways I can use my communication channels as vehicles to promote my work—without being spammy about it, of course.

THOUGHT ANCHORING

Let me know what you think about this conversation.

Me: "I have this great tool that will help you aggregate all of your sales reports and add them up so that you don't have to do data entry ever again."

Random Author: "Whoa! Sign me up!"

Me: "Cool. I just need you to run this Excel macro, wait 10 minutes, and you'll be amazed."

Random Author: "Excel macro....? Nope. See you later."

Me: "Don't run away. Trust me on this. I've simplified it so that all you have to do is click a couple buttons. No code required."

Random Author: "Really?"

Me: "Think about it like this. Isn't the process of uploading a book to Amazon, Kobo, Google, etc. complicated?"

Random Author: "Sometimes."

Me: "If you can upload a book to six different retailers, then you can click a few buttons on my Excel spreadsheet."

What's wrong with the conversation above?

Have you ever been pitched a course by an online marketer, and they say something like "Normally, I'd sell this course for

$600, but because I'm not doing this for the money, I'm charging only $200. People told me I'm nuts for doing this."

That's price anchoring. Give people a higher price and then they will keep referring to that when you give them the lower one. They automatically think the lower price is a better deal, when it's just a marketing tactic.

You can do that with thoughts too.

In marketing my book sales database product, I started way too technical and scared people off.

What I should have started with was "You're an author. You get 10-15 sales reports every month, and what are you supposed to do with them? I surveyed a bunch of writers who told me that they spend an average of 4-5 hours doing their sales reports each month. What if I told you I built a tool that will take all your sales reports, roll them together, add everything up, and give you one report that will tell you how much money you made and how many books you sold?"

Yeah, not my finest marketing moment. I'm not hard on myself, though, even though I squandered an opportunity to sell the product to a gigantic influencer in the self-publishing space. My explanation scared them off.

You live and you learn. Every product is different and you have to find the right way to message it.

GAUGING PAIN LEVELS

Jim Kukral, former host of the *Sell More Books Show*, always said, "If you've got a toothache, what's your pain level?" How bad will you let something get before you go to the dentist?

The general wisdom is that if people's pain level is high, they're more willing to do something about a problem they're facing. If you have a product that solves their pain, they're more likely to buy it.

However, there is such a thing as a friction level.

If a person's pain is a 10 out of 10, and they encounter a solution that will solve 100% of their problem, but it's too difficult to implement, they won't do it. They'll live with the pain because there's too much friction.

Imagine you're on the verge of bankruptcy, and I offer to give you a million dollars. It will solve all your money problems forever. However, in order to get the money, you have to receive ten root canals at the same time. Most people would choose bankruptcy.

I learned this first-hand when building my book sales database. I shared the idea with about 10 different major influencers in the industry in addition to my audience. No matter how I pitched the product, I couldn't get people excited about the problem, even though they admitted that tracking their sales reports was a major problem for them.

I had to learn how to reduce the friction, or rather, give the *perception* that friction didn't exist.

Marketing is Like Going to the Eye Doctor

I've learned that sometimes your marketing doesn't connect and you have to keep shifting the message.

When I built my royalty database, that's what I called it—a royalty database.

I showed it to a fellow influencer, and he didn't get it. Even though he admitted it would have been immensely helpful, it looked scary to him.

I showed it to another influencer, but this time, I made the demo less technical. It still looked scary, but she saw the potential and gave me good advice.

Feeling more confident, I showed it to three more influencers, and instead pitched it as a way to "automate your monthly royalties."

Influencer 3 loved it and offered me money on the spot.

Influencer 4 loved it and put me in contact with her assistant to discuss logistics.

Influencer 5 gave me the advice that made me realize my mistake: "It's interesting. I do think people would want this—at least those who understand what you are talking about."

I discovered that no matter how well I simplified it—and trust me, I oversimplified this damn database—it either scared or confused people.

I stopped talking about Excel. I stopped talking about databases. Instead, I called it the "Author Income Dojo." It's the place where you go to kick your sales reports' asses.

Let me ask you this: what's your most popular book?

What did you earn on that book last month?

What have you earned on that book year-to-date? Is it profitable?

If you can't immediately answer these questions, you're not alone. I mean, let's face it: you probably publish your books on many retailers and you get a ton of sales spreadsheets every month. You don't have time to read them because your time is best spent writing.

What if I told you that I built a tool that takes all your sales spreadsheets, combines them, and gives you amazing insights to your book sales?

Throughout this chapter, I kept shifting the message, much like when you go to the eye doctor and they ask you, "Which looks clearer? One or two?"

I learned to be persistent with my messaging.

JUST KEEP TALKING

Sometimes, people don't act on your message because you didn't refine your message, or because you didn't have the right messaging, or because you caught them at the wrong time, or because they were having a bad week, or because they were too busy, or because they just lost a family member, or because you were ahead of your time, or because you were behind your time and therefore ahead of your time for when people find renewed interest in your subject matter, or because...

You'll never truly know why, though some wonderful readers will tell you what they think occasionally.

But if you keep talking about the book you believe in, eventually, people will pay attention.

I learned this lesson first-hand in my professional life at work this year, where I am an insurance consultant who specializes in insuring the restaurant industry.

It's amazing how quickly circumstances can change.

Restaurant owners resisted things like self-service kiosks, contactless ordering, and artificial intelligence to serve their patrons. They didn't understand why the technology was needed.

Most restaurant owners would have told you, "Wait a minute. You're telling *me* that I should de-incentivize people from coming into my restaurant by telling them to order at a kiosk? You think I should develop a mobile phone app that senses when my customer is approaching so I can give them a special, or ping them on their way home with a coupon so they'll swing by? Are you kidding me? Where am I going to get the money for that, and how can you prove it will work?"

And they would have been right...before COVID-19. Prior to the virus, restaurants were all about in-person experiences—good waiters, good decor, a nice atmosphere, and so on. Those things are irrelevant in a time of social distancing.

If I was a startup trying to get people to buy my contactless ordering software before the pandemic and getting nowhere, I'd be doing a lot more talking during the pandemic era.

Circumstances change, often in ways you can't imagine. That's why you have to keep talking and marketing, even if it's hard.

THOUGHTFUL QUESTIONS

So much in life is all about asking the right questions.

Seth Godin is great at ending his blog posts with a thought-provoking question.

Once, he was talking about the coronavirus and how difficult it is to concentrate during the pandemic. He ended the post with "When it's all over, what will you have done and contributed?"

Throughout the day, I reflected on that question and answered it for myself. Then I wrote a blog post with some words of encouragement for my audience and asked them the same question. A few people commented and said it was exactly the post they needed to read.

Thoughtful questions are a great way to plant seeds in your readers' heads, but also a great tool for engagement.

What's the question you need to ask your readers today?

BECOME A TECHNOLOGY-DRIVEN WRITER

PERSONAL THANK-YOU VIDEOS

I celebrate when people buy my courses. Of all the content I create, I consider it the best compliment when someone likes me and my content enough to buy one of my courses.

I discovered a neat little mobile app called Bonjoro that allows you to send a personal video to someone. They receive an email notification and can watch it in their browser.

I started sending personal thank-you videos to everyone who signed up for my courses. In the video, I say their name, tell them thank you, and that if they have any questions to email me. I give the link to my contact form.

Fifty percent of my customers were floored. The other fifty percent probably never saw the videos because of spam filters.

Sure, this kind of thing isn't scalable, but it's a free and easy way to show your audience that you appreciate them.

LOCALIZED LINKS MAKE YOU MORE MONEY

This lesson is something I've known about for a while, but finally got around to implementing it.

I localized my Amazon links so that the links direct you to the Amazon storefront of the country where you live. It doesn't make sense to send UK readers to Amazon.com if they can't buy from there. They need to be routed to Amazon.co.uk.

Localization also works with the Amazon Associates affiliate program, which is the main reason I implemented the solution.

I know this is simple and likely something everyone knows. But I didn't think spending money on a link localization service made financial sense for me until recently, especially for my fiction book sales alone. My novels receive decent affiliate clicks, but not at a scale to justify $100 per year. However, my YouTube channel is growing, and my increasing affiliate commissions there made me finally take another look at localized link services.

Upon implementing localized links, I saw an instant return on my investment, mainly driven on YouTube by people who bought books I recommended or wanted to know what gear I used. It wasn't anything huge, but I did see a few commissions here and there in other countries that I never would have seen otherwise. Quick math indicated that I would break even on the investment in the first year. If I continue doubling down on YouTube and affiliate links, the service would pay for itself in the second year.

THE POWER OF MIND MAPS

Mind maps are an underappreciated and underutilized tool. I use them all the time for brainstorming.

I happened upon a free course on copyright law from Harvard Law School on YouTube. The professor created an enormous, interactive mind map outlining the essential concepts of copyright law. He shared it for free. I often refer to it when I am reading copyright cases for leisure. You can find it at www.authorlevelup.com/harvardcopyright.

I was intrigued by the idea. A mind map is powerful because it is a *map of your mind*. It's the equivalent of showing your work in algebra class—you are showing someone your thought process around an idea.

How often do people share their thought processes in a transparent way? For example, if you want to know how someone is successful, you have to study their lives and recreate the path. You'll often find gaps. But what if that person shared mind maps that served as snapshots on their journey? Something as trivial as an everyday decision could shed great insight into how that person thinks when they are more successful and you want to study their path.

I experimented with mind maps in this vein, but I haven't come up with anything that was worthy of sharing yet. However, as I explore futurism more, I think it's a perfect way to convey long-term thinking and visualize the future of writing.

COMMAFUL: WATTPAD FOR THE NEXT GENERATION

I had the pleasure of collaborating with Commaful, the world's largest multimedia storytelling app. Young people love it, and teenagers between the age of 13-17 comprise the biggest demographic of the app's user base. The app is similar to Wattpad in that users can write stories, but they can add interactive backgrounds, images, and GIFs. The stories read like little text movies, and the platform makes Wattpad look like your grandpa's writing site. I couldn't help but wonder if this is the distant future of writing. It's a novel app but part of what I believe is a bigger trend of easy-to-create, more interactive multimedia content.

Commaful wants to foster and encourage writing so they invited me to produce a couple writing advice videos for their blog.

Prior to making the videos, I spent a weekend with the app, trying to see what advice writers on the platform needed. I made a story of my own and shared it on social media. Then I realized that the app could be an incredible way to make a text-driven book trailer because you can create one in minutes and embed it on social media. Viewers don't have to have the Commaful app to see your story.

It's always a good idea to see what young people are into, because their likes will manifest themselves in the future, whether you like it or not.

AUDIOGRAMS

I have been listening to podcasts since 2008. I was a podcast listener before it was cool, before Apple launched its podcast app, before all the Internet marketers jumped on the bandwagon, before *Serial*, and before Google announced that it would start indexing podcasts in search results.

A challenge with podcasts has always been how to share them. Audio used to be so expensive to host and stream that you had to hope people had enough patience (and bandwidth) to listen to your show.

In recent years, I've seen podcasters use YouTube and Soundcloud to share snippets of their shows on social media. Now I'm seeing more people use audiograms, which are audio snippets that promote the show, usually with a visualized waveform so that viewers have something to see while they're listening. Podcasting services such as Anchor offer an easy audiogram creation tool, and there is a company called Audiogram that specializes in this technology.

It's hard not to see Google offering something like this in their search results. Audiograms may be how Google serves audio content in the future, cutting up snippets of podcasts it thinks are relevant to a given search—much like what happens with video searches where Google returns 1-2 minutes of a relevant YouTube video that might answer your question. This could potentially disintermediate the podcasting format as we know it, making podcasting truly mainstream while reducing people's attention spans, driving a trend toward shorter content. It would be cataclysmic for long-term podcast listeners like me, but it's probably the future. I'm ready for it.

MERGING EMAIL AND TO-DO LIST

At the time of this writing, I receive 1,200 emails per month, which is around 40 per day. Most days, I can manage the volume, but when I fall behind, it can take me weeks to catch up.

I tend to change my email client like you change the arrangement of furniture in your living room—once every few years.

This year, I experimented with an email client that mixed email with a to-do list. I'm not a huge to-do list fan, but I found an app called Sortd that provides the best of both worlds. It's not perfect, but it did help me stay productive for a while.

DATABASE INTEGRATION: ONE TRUTH

I got tired of filling out marketing forms and having to put the same information about my books into them every time. When you're marketing your book, it's staggering how many times you need links, ASINs, book descriptions, and so on. You have to input this information into contact forms, your website, and more. I often forget little things like price or trim size, and I find myself looking them up often, which takes too long.

I decided to build a book database in Microsoft Access that houses all of the information for my books so that I can keep everything in a central location. Any time I have questions about my book details, I fire up the database. I can even export data in any form I want to.

I still have to copy and paste, which is tedious, but the database is just the first step in a long-term strategy.

The database can also become the engine for my website. Imagine loading a book into the database, and then pushing it to your website. Your website would then auto-create a page for your book, with all of the correct information, populated from the database, with the ability to update it as needed. This is absolutely possible—I used to work for a web development company and we did SQL server integrations for clients all the time. My next website iteration will have this functionality.

Next, imagine a browser extension that pulls from your database and auto-populates forms with your book information. All you have to do is choose which book it populated and verify that the information on the form is correct. This would save you time when you're marketing the book or sharing it on social media.

Next, imagine entering your book into a database and then being able to publish your book to book retailers from the database instead of signing in to a dashboard. That technology exists; traditional publishers use it every day. It's the future for indie authors. More successful and prolific writers will demand it. Distributors like PublishDrive recognize this need and already quietly offer bulk uploads and database integration so that you can publish by uploading a specially-formatted ONIX file.

As I scale my business, it's increasingly important to maintain fewer records with more accurate data. One day, when I have over 100 books, I need one version of the truth that preferably serves as a Swiss Army knife for whatever I need it to do.

Building my database was the first step in that future I want to create for myself.

EXCEL MACROS

I've always been afraid of Microsoft Excel. Its interface isn't suited to my thinking style. I don't consider myself as someone who has strong data analysis skills, but I'm trying to improve.

When I built my book sales report database, I threw my fears aside and dove into learning it.

I took interactive Excel courses, watched hours of Excel videos on YouTube, and read Excel books. I even learned how to write Visual Basic for Applications (VBA)—something that makes most people run away screaming. As part of my sales database project, I wrote over 10,000 lines of VBA code that worked very well. I also hired a few programmers to help me with the most difficult parts, and they taught me a lot.

I learned that macros, while scary, are amazingly useful. They save time by helping you automate mundane and repetitive tasks.

Sales reports are the definition of mundane and repetitive. I don't know anyone who enjoys digging through them. I created macros that manipulated sales reports from multiple retailers into something more palatable that you can use to make data-driven decisions about your sales. I created the tool for myself but found that others can use it too.

I harnessed the power of macros and automation, and my business is much better for it. I now have access to more data, so I can improve my data analysis skills.

Not bad for a guy who barely knew what a macro was before he started the project.

SOMETIMES, YOU JUST CAN'T HELP PEOPLE

This chapter isn't what you think it is—a rant about human nature and some writers' indomitable stubbornness and inability to accept that they have flaws...

Instead, I'm talking about book and product development.

Every once in a while, you get this amazing idea to solve a problem.

Maybe you write a book that, on paper, is the sweet spot in an underserved fiction genre.

Or maybe you come up with a unique nonfiction book or course that helps your audience do something.

There will be a time when you simply can't help the people you want to because of factors out of your control.

Maybe the idea is too expensive or too technical for the average person. Or maybe you can't reach the people you want to reach because it's too difficult to find them.

In any case, you have a choice: keep moving forward and hope you'll succeed, which isn't likely, or you stop and abandon the project.

I ran into this problem with my sales report tool, Author Income Dojo.

I was tired of dealing with complicated sales reports every month and I wanted a simpler solution. I scoured the planet for a solution, and I wouldn't stop until I found one.

I did, and I wanted to share it with the community.

While it was a complete solution for me, it was a partial solution for others.

Essentially, it worked perfectly for Windows users, but for Mac users, it involved installing Windows on your Mac.

Yikes.

I tried to develop an alternative solution for Mac users, but I couldn't make it work even after consulting with two Microsoft Certified MVPs.

Macs just aren't built for the type of tool I created, and there was nothing I could do about it.

As a result, I couldn't help the average Mac user in my community.

Asking people to install Windows on their computers is a big ask.

This was an example of not being able to help people. It happens a lot, unfortunately.

THE DANGERS OF WEB SCRAPING

This year, I partnered with a Silicon Valley-based developer to build a tool that could help me with my writing business. It involved data mining and web scraping, and it would have been a game-changer for me, and possibly the writing community. We didn't pursue the project for legal reasons.

Web scraping is when a "bot" takes information off a website and provides it to the owner for any number of reasons, mainly for competitive intelligence.

Companies like Amazon and Google didn't like web scraping back in the old days because it caused problems for their servers. This is why Amazon, Google, and major websites offer Application Programming Interfaces (APIs). An API is like a plug-socket arrangement where your program is the plug and the website is the socket. When you connect to an API, you agree that your bots will follow certain protocols and rules. Companies provide data in exchange for your bots playing nice with their servers.

The problem with our project was that we could use APIs, but our particular use case was not technically a sanctioned use of the APIs. That left us with the choice to use the APIs for our purposes and hope we wouldn't get caught, or to scrape data from them, which was also against most sites' terms of service. Both choices were unpalatable.

Compulife Software, Inc. v. Newman, **F.3d** , 2020 WL 2549505, (*11th Cir. May 20, 2020*) was the kind of case we were worried about. In that case, the plaintiff compiled insurance company rates that were publicly available and then wrapped them into a database that it then provided to customers to get life insurance quotes, I presume as a comparative rater so customers could get multiple quotes from different companies at the same time.

The defendants, Compulife's competitors, created bots that scraped the database to discern the workings of Compulife's proprietary product, which was protected as a trade secret.

Normally, if a hacker did this, they would glean some important data, but a key fact in this case is that the bots were able to scrape 42 million computations of the potential data in the database, giving the defendant an immense competitive advantage and the ability to reverse engineer what Compulife had created.

In my case, the web scraping was innocent and for my own commercial use.

In the Compulife case, the scraping was nefarious.

You can see how the same technology can be used for both good and evil.

The programmers and I left the project at "this is a really messy legal issue right now, but the courts and legislature will have to address it at some point because APIs are the future. If average people can't use APIs to get data that they own, that's not the world we want to live in." We didn't like the legal and ethical crossroads we found ourselves at.

Not only was our decision the correct one, it was right on time given the Compulife case, which came out soon after we halted the project.

Is something a trade secret if it's based on publicly available information?

You may be wondering why I care about this.

Well, the information on a book retailer's website is public, isn't it? For example, your book's metadata can be scraped easily off Amazon, and also obtained through Amazon's Product Advertising API. How would you feel if someone could access the information about all your books that is available publicly and use the data to gain a business advantage over you? (News flash: they already can.)

And couldn't one argue that retailers don't own that data, that it's merely facts created by authors? *Shouldn't* authors have a right to gather their own facts and use them for whatever purpose they desire?

In the insurance industry, insurance agents have "agency management systems" that allow them to manage their customer accounts with different insurance companies. The software is a customer database that downloads insurance rates and policies and allows the agent to make changes to the customer's policies.

Why don't authors have "book management systems" that do the same thing with their books? Why log in to a retailer's dashboard when you can log in to a database on your computer that communicates with the book retailer instead?

In short, authors are going to need more access to data about their books in the future to make business decisions. Retailers have that data, but they limit our access to it. When I think about who might disrupt Big Tech like Amazon and Google, I think of companies whose business model is democratizing data (ironically, which is how the Big Tech companies started, but they hoard data now). That, or evolving technology and market forces, will push Big Tech to grant access to more data via APIs.

This project was another example where I was ahead of my time.

TEXT SPINNER AI

A text spinner is software that takes a source text, modifies it slightly, and produces new material that someone can then pass off as their own. Text spinners are used all the time for plagiarism.

Using a text spinner is also clearly copyright infringement. However, if the software used AI, it prompts the question of who owns the copyright to the spun material.

This issue came up when Pamela DuMond, a bestselling romance author, sued author Emma Chase over copyright infringement. DuMond alleged that her romantic comedy novel, *Part-Time Princess*, was copied by author Emma Chase, whose romantic comedy novel is *Royally Screwed*, published by Simon & Schuster.

In addition to copyright infringement, DuMond and her attorneys alleged that Chase and Simon & Schuster used text spinning software to write *Royally Screwed*.

The complaint contains very convincing side-by-side comparisons of both novels, showing plot points, passages, and even character names that are a little too similar to be a coincidence.

If the allegations are true, this is potentially a bombshell case. Did Chase use the text spinning software before submitting the novel to Simon & Schuster? If so, why didn't the publisher's team catch it? Didn't they practice due diligence? Wasn't there a warranty clause in the publishing contract that says the author warrants that the work doesn't infringe on anyone's copyrights, and a hold harmless and indemnification clause that stipulates that the author will hold the publisher harmless for any claims arising from copyright infringement? These are boilerplate clauses in any publishing contract that typically can't be negotiated away. If those clauses are present in the publishing contract, then why is Simon & Schuster defending the case instead of cutting ties with the author and asking to be dismissed from the lawsuit? Wouldn't allegations of plagiarism (especially by software) run contrary to the publisher's brand, and therefore be toxic to them? Why are they doubling down on their legal defense team?

Or...did Simon & Schuster's staff use the software? Who used it, who condoned it, what did all of those people know and when did they know it? Did the CEO know? Are other big publishers doing this? If so, who else have they plagiarized?

And more pragmatically—who owns the copyright to the infringing material? The publisher or the AI?

These are all allegations, of course, and I'm not making any accusations. I'm simply asking the questions. But something smells funny. Good attorneys are like bloodhounds—they'll uncover the truth.

This case, while still young at the time of this writing, has earthquake potential on the level of the big publisher price-fixing collusion lawsuit in 2009.

The Passive Guy did a great analysis of the case on his blog and he opined that it could also shape the future of how copyright infringement cases are tried. It would also have broader implications on text spinner software and copyright ownership.

I don't know the answers, but it's an interesting problem.

PUBLISHED BOOKS ARE REAL ESTATE

Your published books are like real estate. They need to be managed just like a landlord manages their properties.

A good landlord always knows what's going on at their properties. They know if pipes are leaking, what dates someone is moving in or out, or when a roof needs to be updated.

Do you know what's going on with your book on Kobo right now? What categories is it in? How about Google Play? What's the discounted price Google is selling your book at right now?

Exactly. You probably don't know. I didn't either, until this year.

Many authors think about the management of their published books as an administrative problem—one that is solved manually or by an assistant. I suggest that this is not an administrative problem; it's a data problem.

The best way to manage your books is to condense them into data points. Look for issues with the data points and manage them accordingly.

To use a simple example, if your book's price should be $2.99, but it's $3.99 at one retailer, that's a problem you can easily solve if you aggregate all your prices into one place to review them. The wrong price will stick out. We can solve this problem and others like it with data tools like Excel and Access, or long-term, dedicated software.

It took a long time for the indie community to think about books as products. I also believe it will be important to think about our books as data too.

BECOME A DATA-DRIVEN
WRITER

CLEAN AND MESSY DATA

Our goal is clean data. But when data comes to us, it's often messy.

Think about the sales reports you receive every month. They're not exactly easy to read.

I struck a friendship with a Microsoft Excel MVP, who is one of the top Excel experts in the world. Businesses pay him to consult on data problems, and he makes a good living at it. I learned a lot from chatting with him.

In order to get data clean, we have to do what data analyst professionals call "data wrangling," "data cleansing," or "data munging." This means cleaning up headers, deleting unnecessary data, converting currencies, and so much more so we can get our sales reports to a readable state.

So if we wanted to clean up our sales reports, we'd find a way to standardize them so that they're easier to read, say the same thing, and can be connected. We can do this in many ways, but Microsoft Excel is the tool that can help us do it most effectively.

Without clean data, you can't make decisions, just like you can't see through a dusty window.

EASY DATA ANALYSIS QUESTIONS

I was fortunate enough to have a mentor at work this year who helped me improve my data analysis skills. The mentor taught me to ask a couple of basic questions when looking at any dataset.

What is the data saying at first glance?

Where are the outliers?

If you look "under the covers," what do the outliers tell you?

Does this data make sense given what we know?

What data isn't here?

How do we validate what *is* here?

These are all basic questions, but they helped me make sure I was approaching a work project with a difficult data set correctly.

YOUTUBE ANALYTICS LESSONS

I've learned a lot about my YouTube audience, which has evolved rapidly over the last year as I've brought on new subscribers.

Sixty percent of my audience is age 25-44.

About 40% of my audience is female, but they tend to be more engaged in the content and therefore post more often.

About 20-30% of my views are from outside the United States, with many watching me from the United Kingdom, Canada, Germany, and surprisingly, India.

A sizable percentage of my audience is people of color, but I can't quantify that.

Many in my audience are aspiring writers or have published a handful of books. Most are indie.

My YouTube subscribers like me best when I am exploring writing app technology, sharing transparent stories about my journey, or doing deep dives into fiction craft. When I stray away from those, my YouTube stats suffer.

I've learned to find the sweet spot between content I want to produce versus content my audience wants. This year, I learned to shift non-marketable topics on my podcast, *The Writer's Journey*, where my listeners are more open to listening to unusual ideas. With YouTube, I will stay in my sweet spots, which, fortunately, align with my passions right now.

POWER QUERY

Owning a Mac has many advantages. Doing data analysis isn't one of them.

I didn't know Excel Power Query existed until this year because the Mac version of Excel doesn't have it.

Wow, is it powerful!

Hook up Excel Power Query and Microsoft Access with Microsoft Power BI, and you'll have a data analysis engine that is unrivaled in the indie community. To do this, you have to run Windows 10 on a virtual machine if you own a Mac, however.

If you have no idea what I just said, look it up. You'll thank me for showing you that you've been doing "data" wrong your whole life.

DATABASE NORMALIZATION RULES

This lesson may sound like Greek, or it may not. Let's give it a try, shall we?

In learning database management, the first thing I learned was the fundamental concept of database normalization, which is a universally-accepted approach to building and maintaining databases. The following three rules will ensure that you lay a good foundation for your database.

It's best to think of a database as a series of interconnected tables. Each table should be tall and narrow, meaning they only store the minimum amount of data that is needed.

Rule 1NF states that each cell should only contain a single value. For example, instead of a full name, there should be two fields, one for the first and last name.

Rule 2NF states that data not dependent on the primary key should be moved to a separate table. The primary key is a unique identifier on a particular table that links it to other tables in the database. An employee ID is a classic example of a primary key. An employee ID identifies a name, title, address, and possibly more—and each of those items are stored in separate tables. If you have a table that represents which of your employees helped which of your customers, there should be one table for employees and one for customers; this way, you can link the tables together rather than storing everything on one table. The primary key for each table might be an employee ID and customer ID, respectively.

Rule 3NF states that data that can be derived from other fields should not be stored. For example, on the employee table, you shouldn't store a field for employee initials. You can calculate that with an equation using the employees' first and last name fields.

Anyway, these were the ground rules I followed when building my book database.

Maybe it can help you at some point in your journey.

DATABASES ARE COPYRIGHTABLE

People copyright databases all the time. It's not terribly helpful for most people to know this, but it was helpful for me when I was building my book database because I now understand the true sales and licensing potential.

ONIX, METADATA, AND DATABASES

I have a subscription to LinkedIn Learning and happened to encounter a course on metadata and book publishing.

The course was like the Matrix. It validated all of my database work. It turns out that traditional publishers also manage their books in databases. They use an industry-standard markup language called ONIX, which stands for Online Information Exchange. An ONIX file contains all of a book's or books' metadata and stores it in a special format so that publishers can, with a click of a button, send their books to distributors, retailers, bookstores, and other trading partners.

I always thought there was some poor soul at a publishing house who had to upload and manage the publishers' books on various dashboards. That's not how it works, at least for large publishers.

ONIX is generally exclusive to traditional publishing circles, but the truth is that indie authors can use it too.

In fact, the book database I developed was a crude version of ONIX without realizing it.

Then I discovered through the course that there is professional metadata management software that was designed to help publishers manage this problem. It costs less than $100 (at the time of this writing).

That's when I realized: why develop my own format when I can use the industry standard?

By adopting the industry standard, I can integrate a future database more easily with my website and also bulk upload my titles to a future retailer without any additional effort.

Learning about ONIX was a critical step in my database journey.

DATA DOESN'T GET WRITERS EXCITED

I've doubled down on learning data analysis this year, but I learned that most writers don't want anything to do with data. It scares them. I get it.

How can one motivate people to get excited about data? I believe it's possible if you show them the benefits and give them a tool that helps them bypass the worst part of data analysis, which are data entry and data cleaning. I think many authors would actually be pretty good at data analysis if you visualized it for them. It's not hard; the challenge is getting to the visualization, which requires a few steps. Every step is friction.

POWER BI AND DASHBOARDS

While working on my sales database tool, I discovered Microsoft's Power BI product. BI stands for business intelligence. Outside of data analyst and data science circles, few people know what Power BI is or that it even exists.

You can feed data into Power BI and visualize it in sophisticated yet easy-to-create dashboards. You can create any chart or graph you can dream of, for less time and effort than it would take you in Excel. For example, I can visualize all of my book sales on a geographic map. Some book retailers collect the states, provinces, or ZIP codes of their readers. In the United States, I can see what cities and states my readers are from; for Canada, I can see what territories my readers live in. That's very, very useful.

After building my sales report database, I fed it into Power BI and created a visual dashboard that showed my sales data in an instantly understandable format. It's an indispensable tool, one that I can use for all areas of my business, not just book sales.

Imagine hiring a developer to help you integrate your book sales, website analytics, email newsletter statistics, and any other metric you need to track onto an organized dashboard on Power BI, using APIs and (legal) web scraping. Imagine waking up with a monthly digest of your vital business data. Wouldn't that be a game-changer? That's what I'll be working on in the future.

I have been saying that learning database technology is possibly the biggest breakthrough I have made in my business since publishing my first book. A sound database is the Swiss Army knife for the writer of the future.

RANSOM ATTACKS: A GROWING THREAT

Ransom attacks are on the rise. I talk about this exposure at length in my course *Writing in Hard Times*. I believe it is an emerging threat for writers, but I don't talk about it publicly for fear of bad guys hearing it.

A ransomware attack is when a cybercriminal gets access to your computer and then shuts it down and makes you pay money to get access back.

Many people think ransomware attacks only happen at large organizations. I've read industry statistics that somewhere around 60-70% of ransomware attacks are actually on small businesses.

Writers are small businesses. In fact, we're what the industry calls "micro small businesses."

It's just a matter of time before ransomware creators realize that self-published writers are worthy targets, so start preparing now.

The average ransom for a large business is somewhere between $100,000 and $400,000. For self-published writers, I imagine that the ransom would be a couple hundred dollars. Why? Because the bad guys want to make sure you can pay the ransom. Their entire business model (if you want to call it that) is predicated on their marks paying them.

If a ransom attack happens to you, you have three choices.

First, you can try to disinfect the computer yourself using Internet research or by hiring a computer technician.

Second, you can pay the ransom.

Third, you can abandon the computer.

None of those choices are ideal, so make sure your work is backed up to alternative sources so you have more flexibility.

I'll link to two informative videos I found while researching this topic for my *Writing in Hard Times* course that will help educate you on this topic. You can find them at www.author levelup.com/ransom

AI IS COOL, BUT IT'S ALSO SCARILY DECEPTIVE

Few emerging technologies hold promise like artificial intelligence and machine learning.

Many people are placing blind faith in artificial intelligence, hoping that it will eventually solve many business problems.

The writing community is no different. Perhaps the biggest impact that AI and machine learning can make is in editing. Imagine not having to hire a copyeditor in the future, but instead running your book through a sophisticated algorithm that catches most major errors. That will be a reality one day.

But not today.

You can see AI at work in Microsoft Office. PowerPoint will recommend ideas for slide designs based on your content; Excel will show you data based on questions you ask it; Outlook will show you emails that need attention.

Grammarly, the ubiquitous grammar app, is driven by artificial intelligence and machine learning. So are your smart speakers. All the aforementioned technology is promising, but it's still too new to drive true efficiency.

Most AI applications I have seen for writers have been basic at best, but the marketing makes them look better than they are.

A friend of mine is a Microsoft Excel MVP and he warned me about how AI and ML in Excel in particular is new and prone to mistakes and false positives.

That said, I believe it's very, very important *not* to dismiss emerging technology based on its quality. Think about how many people laughed at the first iPhone because it was slow compared to "dumb" phones at the time. Who's laughing at the iPhone now?

Quality is a red herring that distracts people from the real reason the technology exists.

I consulted on a project to build a custom app for writers this year. In my conversations with the developers (who were extremely talented), I learned that artificial intelligence needs massive amounts of data to be successful. A data engineer can't just build an AI algorithm. They need to feed the AI engine, and that engine is like a coal furnace. Someone's got to constantly feed the beast.

All that data has to come from somewhere. Therefore, companies make their apps available for free to the public with a façade of helping people solve simple tasks, but with the real goal of aggregating data to make the AI engine more effective.

The conversations I had with folks around AI behind closed doors were eye-opening, and a little frightening.

The next time you see a glitzy new app that promises to use the power of AI to help you succeed in life, first ask yourself what data it is taking from you. Second, ask yourself how they're going to use it. Third, consider the very real possibility of whether this company will be around in five years or if they will be sold or acquired—along with your data. Fourth, consider for what reason they might be acquired. If you can step through that mental exercise and come to an answer, you now understand the company's true motive. Then, make your decision accordingly on whether the app is truly worth your time.

Understand that the quality may not be where you expect it to be, but that quality is a red herring. History shows that the quality will *always* improve. The more people use a software with artificial intelligence and machine learning, the smarter it gets over time.

Also, consider this. In the business world, entrepreneurs pitch products to investors. Investors get irritated when an entrepreneur walks through the door with no experience in the industry they're entering. The entrepreneur wants the investors' help and contacts to learn the market.

As a general rule, investors don't like to pay to educate entrepreneurs. It's expensive and usually doesn't end well.

Are YOU okay giving away your data —which has immense value, by the way—to help train an AI with no real benefit in return?

With AI services, you are an investor, and you must choose where and with whom to spend your data.

Remember that when AI becomes more prevalent in the publishing community.

I'm a strong proponent for AI, but I do worry that writers won't truly understand the technology and its risks when bad actors are involved.

BECOME THE WRITER OF
THE FUTURE

ALIGN YOUR BUDGET WITH YOUR PRIORITIES

This year, I spoke frequently on all my communication channels about my 2020 and beyond strategy.

My five strategic priorities are to become a world-class content creator, to become a world-class marketer, to become a technology-driven writer, to become a data-driven writer, and to become the writer of the future.

Every project I take on fits into one of those categories.

To cement my strategy further, I revised my budget for 2021 to align with my strategic priorities. This way, I'm putting my money where my mouth is.

How much do I allot for each priority? That was an interesting mental exercise, but necessary. I decided that for the next two to three years, I need to invest more money in data, technology, and futuristic items because we are currently in hard economic times. Looking ahead, I want to emerge from this period with significant advantages. In two to three years, more of my budget will shift toward production and marketing.

FOUR AREAS AI CAN HELP WRITERS

One of the things I have enjoyed most this year is learning about artificial intelligence. I've had conversations with some smart people who have given me great advice.

As I look at the indie publishing community, I think there are four major areas where AI can help us.

The first area is a replacement for developmental editing. Before you come to my house with an angry mob, hear me out...

There are already companies that offer AI developmental editing software. They work by comparing your manuscript to bestselling books. While the quality is questionable *today*, remember my prior comments about quality for emerging technology. It's a red herring. At some point, the quality will improve and there will be a company that wins in the space. This kind of technology will render developmental editors irrelevant, though it won't eliminate the profession.

If you can pay software less than $100 to glean insights about your story's weaknesses, why would you pay several thousand to an editor to do the same thing?

Quality is irrelevant. The main reason that authors pay for developmental editors today is because there's no other good alternative. If they have a choice between an expensive editor and affordable software that is *good enough*, they'll choose the software. Also consider that many authors who hire developmental editors are new and aspiring writers, who, ironically, have the least money to spend because they don't have book sales yet.

The same is true with copyediting and proofreading, but I think the horizon for AI replacing a copyeditor is much further away. It is extraordinarily difficult to program the rules of English into software. Many have tried; most have failed. So far.

The second area is writing assistance. AI has the potential to help us become better versions of ourselves. I don't need AI software that gives me generic spelling and grammar recommendations. I *do* need software that can look at all of the mistakes I've made in my past writing and help me avoid making them again. That would save me editing costs and help me create cleaner books. AI models need a lot of data, so this isn't likely possible until someone finds a way to generate better models that require less data.

Further out, imagine integration with biohacking technology. What if my writing app could track my vitals during writing sessions and tell me when it's time to stop writing because I'm too tired? Or maybe it could sense when I'm distracted and gently redirect me to another function in my writing business instead where my attention would be more productive, like marketing? If I ignored it and wrote anyway, the app could mark those sections with a recommendation for my editor to pay more attention to them and why. It would know my error rate and compare that to my vitals over time. In a sense, your writing app could assume a function similar to a nurse. Your editor would become more like a (true) book doctor, treating areas of the manuscript that are most problematic. In the future, if the book has been run through developmental editing software and more sophisticated grammar and spellchecker software based on prior mistakes, an editor's approach will have to be different and more holistic.

The third area is marketing assistance. Marketing today is manual. I believe AI can help.

Amazon Advertising (and pay-per-click advertising in general) for example, is an area where AI can make a big difference in authors' lives. Every decision with ads is data-driven. If you give a human and an AI a data-driven decision, the AI will win (almost) every time. I love the idea of running my ad reports through an AI that can recommend things like daily budgets, keywords, categories, and so on.

Your first instinct to this might be, "If everyone uses AI for their ads, then they'll become less effective." I don't think that's true. Every book has its own unique audience. We already know that authors aren't truly competitors. If you and I write similar books, readers will eventually want to read them both because they want content that is more similar than different.

Pay-per-click advertising is a discovery tool, so if advanced software can help you get your books discovered, it could help with the discoverability problem and make the "long tail" of book discovery fatter, which means that authors who sell almost no copies of their work can find a bigger audience. Multiply this across the entire industry and you have a bonanza if a developer can get this right.

I also think about software that can monitor any activity around you and your books on the Internet, and provide that to you as a daily report, like Google Alerts but way more powerful. It can send bots to every corner of the Internet, across search engines, podcasts, video sites, and retailers to see what people are saying about you and your books. Maybe it employs sentiment analysis so it knows what's positive and what's negative.

Amazon already uses this technology in its product reviews section.

The fourth area is writing to market. It takes a lot of time to figure out where your book fits in a given market. I do extensive market research, but it seems like no matter how hard I work, I always miss a few books that are similar to mine. It would be nice if AI could do market research. It doesn't have to be right one hundred percent of the time, but if it can make connections that I wouldn't have made otherwise, it's worth it.

There are other ways AI can help indie authors, to be sure, but these are the major areas I am interested in.

BRANDON SANDERSON
KICKSTARTER

Many people are celebrating Brandon Sanderson's Kickstarter to create a leather bound edition of one of his books, which funded in minutes and made him several million dollars. It's an amazing success, and I wish him all the best with it.

Dean Wesley Smith argues that it will make Kickstarter pay more attention to publishing projects, which have historically had a high failure rate. Dean has been fairly successful at Kickstarter, integrating it into his regular product creation schedule.

I wonder if that will be a model for the future: write a book, run a Kickstarter to fund limited editions, rinse, and repeat. Kickstarter could become part of your launch strategy, occupying a similar place as Patreon—a fringe revenue source (for most people), but one you can use to drive value for your biggest fans.

DIRECT SALES INTEGRATIONS

I'm finally getting around to integrating direct sales on my website. I've used a few different direct payment services over the years, but I've never been happy with them. They cause too much friction, and the good ones can be expensive.

I used to have a direct store called Michael La Ronn Direct, but I disabled it because it was too much trouble to maintain and readers didn't like it. I decided that I wouldn't do direct sales again until I could do it right.

I rediscovered Payhip, which is affordable and intuitive. They've improved the platform considerably over the years.

My goal is to implement it onto my website by end of the year.

I'm leaving money on the table by not doing direct sales, and I recognize that. There were too many other projects with a better ROI that I kept pushing this down on my priority list. But since this year is an infrastructure year for me, now is the time to implement direct sales again so that I can improve my earnings.

I will also need the ability to accept cryptocurrencies and blockchain transactions in the future, but I'm not ready for that yet.

BACKGROUND ELIMINATOR

An affiliate network I participate in sent me an email about a new affiliate that promised to use AI to eliminate unwanted background noise during conference calls. Crying babies, barking dogs, loud spouses, and so on. The affiliate network promised that the product was a slam dunk for people working from home due to the pandemic, and I bet the claim was true.

The email came at an interesting time because I happened to notice similar technology in other places that week.

Eliminate background noise with the help of artificial intelligence.

Adobe Premiere offers this technology with its sound healing feature. I once watched someone eliminate a telephone ring from a piece of audio. It was as if the ring was never there. This is why Adobe is a pioneer in AI.

Now, this new affiliate offered that same technology, but in real-time. They've probably been in business for a while but are just now starting to get traction. Companies like that don't just come out of nowhere.

Around the time I wrote this chapter, I also happened to be on a Microsoft Teams call; while I was setting up my microphone, I noticed a green screen feature that allowed me to change my background to something more pleasant, like a beach, a fake conference room, or even outer space. While it wasn't a true green screen replacement, it didn't look bad.

Background and background noise replacement in real-time. I believe this is the start of a bigger trend that is going to catch fire in the next few years.

What if a podcast recording app allowed you to eliminate background noise, therefore allowing you to record anywhere, like a busy park or a crowded food court? What if it could make your voice sound better too?

What if a video editing app could replace your background and lighting without the use of a green screen?

In case the trend isn't clear, let me explain.

If you look at the history of audio and video recording, it is all about democratizing the medium so that more people can create in it. Only film broadcasting studios could shoot high quality video until digital cameras came along. Podcasting as we know it today was possible twenty years ago, but only if you had the money to afford sound equipment and the know-how to operate it.

Today, anyone can make high-quality videos on their smartphones; they can use those same smartphones to record podcasts with apps like Anchor.

Now we have a new wave of technology that will make it easier for people to record anywhere without fear of distracting background noise or unprofessional backgrounds. Imagine what this could do in developing countries, or for those people who are too self-conscious to put themselves into the world for fear of loud children or lack of space to create green screen videos.

As the price of smartphones and audio and video decrease and the quality of their signal capture increase, we have more content creators who will feel empowered to make content that they otherwise would have never considered. And that's a good thing.

If the technology quality advances significantly, we might even see a world where people can narrate studio audiobooks thanks to background noise elimination. Is it a stretch? Maybe, but's it interesting.

SUBLICENSES

When you license your copyrights, sometimes the people or companies you license your work to may want to license your work again. The classic example might be a publisher signing a deal on your behalf to get your book into audio.

Whenever possible, you want to control sublicense situations, and you don't want a licensee signing rights on your behalf. This can be negotiated into a licensing contract.

If you're looking at a contract, it may be a useful thought exercise to think about potential situations where a sublicensing situation can come up.

It's also worth thinking about how sublicensing works on the sites you use every day. For example, if you post a photo to Instagram, you're giving Instagram (and anyone who uses it) a license to embed your photo anywhere. What if someone embeds your photo on their website instead of paying you for it, but your photography business is based on licensing your photos for a fee? There was a lawsuit about this very topic this year.

Part of being the writer of the future is understanding how the contracts you sign today will impact your career ten, twenty, or thirty years into the future.

LICENSING YOUR PERSONA

I spoke with a company this year about licensing my voice to read audiobooks. They make AI versions of your voice so that readers can choose who reads their audiobooks to them. The technology is advancing so fast that soon you won't be able to tell it's an AI. It reminds me a lot of when GPSes introduced custom voices like Homer Simpson and Samuel L. Jackson to narrate turn-by-turn directions.

That seems to be where audio is headed—one market for standard, traditionally-narrated audiobooks, and another for cheaper versions narrated by AI.

While the talks with the company didn't work out, I learned a great deal about which direction I need to pivot. I need to create hours and hours of high quality audio narration so that I can put myself in a position to license my voice for this technology. This way, readers can choose to hear my voice narrate ALL of my books, whether I narrated them traditionally or not. There are many interesting opportunities that can spring from this technology.

COPYRIGHT EXPIRATION

I was working with an author to help him publish a book. He wanted my feedback, so I reviewed his cover, book description, and more.

I then noticed that his book was a reimagining of another book that was published in 1926.

The question both of us were curious about was: could he do this?

There were two issues: the first was whether the original book was in the public domain or not. Per the United States Copyright Act, works published prior to 1925 are in the public domain. Works published prior to January 1, 1978 could have been extended 95 years of protection from the publication date if the registration was renewed in the 28th year of publication, but they cannot get more than 95 years of protection from the date of publication.

What I learned in doing a copyright search was that a revised version of the book was registered in the 29th year, so the heir to the author's estate missed the window. From what I could tell, even though the copyright office granted the registration, the book entered the public domain. Only the new and revised parts of the book would have been protected. Even if the book didn't for some reason enter the public domain, it will in 2021.

But the author I was working with didn't copy any of the text from the book, so ultimately, he would have been fine. There was no copyright infringement. We were simply curious.

The second issue, which was the real issue, was whether the book title was trademarked, not as a book title, but as a brand. This was a self-help book. Sometimes self-help gurus will trademark books not as books, but as brands that include books. While you can't trademark a book title, you CAN trademark a brand, which means you can authorize someone to take down a book that has a trademark in the title.

After performing a trademark search, this did not appear to be the case, so the author will probably be fine.

But it begs another thought: it's just a matter of time before the trademark wars reach publishing.

I've been concerned for quite some time about trademark trolls wreaking havoc on merchandise sellers on Etsy and Amazon.

The dangerous part about trademarks is that they work retroactively; if you publish a series today and someone secures a trademark on a series title five years from now, they can make you take your book down or change your series title.

So far, the community has taken a strong stance against authors trying to secure trademarks for series titles. Those efforts have been successful, but someone will break the pattern at some point, creating a watershed moment.

We may eventually reach the point where some authors may have to proactively trademark elements of their work to avoid this problem, which will drive up the cost of publishing. It could create haves and have-nots, where trolls actively trade-mark series titles of successful books by have-nots who can't afford trademarks. The trolls will extort those authors to make money or to silence voices they don't want to be heard.

I hope this future doesn't become a reality.

SHERLOCK AND ENOLA HOLMES

In 2008, author Nancy Springer published a series called *The Enola Holmes Mysteries*. It followed a character she invented named Enola Holmes, who is the fictional sister of Sherlock Holmes. The story follows her as she solves mysteries. Sherlock Holmes, Dr. Watson, and Mycroft Holmes make regular appearances in the stories. The books were so popular that they were adapted into a major motion picture film.

The estate of Sir Arthur Conan Doyle sued for copyright infringement. They sued Springer, Penguin, Netflix, the movie production studios, and the screenwriter and director, alleging copyright *and* trademark infringement.

The character Sherlock Holmes is in the public domain. However, the last ten short stories that Conan Doyle wrote are not. The estate argued that Conan Doyle wrote these stories after World War I, when he decided to change the essence of Sherlock Holmes. Holmes had a reputation for being aloof and somewhat cold; Conan Doyle changed that and made him warmer.

Because the books and film portray Holmes as kind, the estate alleged that the author committed copyright infringement because the Holmes that appears in the Enola Holmes Mysteries exhibits character traits from the latter Holmes, which are still under copyright. They also alleged violation of trademarks around the Sherlock Holmes brand because the name Enola Holmes could create customer confusion and therefore lead consumers to believe that the *Enola Holmes Mysteries* are affiliated with the Conan Doyle estate, which they are not.

There are a lot of moving parts to this case, but the most interesting takeaway for me was the trademark infringement allegations. I've said for the last two to three years that we are going to see more trademark claims against authors—primarily because more authors will start to secure trademarks as a defensive gesture. And once you own a trademark, you have to defend it or you'll lose it. This will create a legal environment where the "haves" can afford to secure trademarks and enforce them while the "have-nots" will have no choice but to acquiesce to any demand because they cannot afford the legal costs.

That is a terrifying future. At least with copyright infringement, you won't be sued unless the other person can make a compelling case against you. There are certain barriers to frivolous lawsuits. Those barriers do not exist with trademarks.

I worry about the precedent a case like this could set if the Conan Doyle estate wins, but at the time of this writing, it's too soon to tell.

Another unspoken element of the case that gave me pause was the contractual arrangement between the author and the publisher, Penguin Random House.

Like the case I explored earlier, I have questions. Did the publisher's legal team not do any kind of due diligence? Or were they confident that if a lawsuit arose, they could afford the risk?

Most importantly, did the author have a hold harmless agreement with the publisher? I'd wager not, especially if

Penguin was aware of the potential conflicts—which they probably were. I can only hope she had a solid contract.

Years ago, my very first novel (which I never finished) borrowed significantly from the public domain. It featured many public domain characters, and I thought the concept was pretty cool. However, I scrapped the project for the very concern that Conan Doyle's estate is suing for now—I worried at the time that copyright might extend to character traits, as not all the characters in the story had bodies of work that were *completely* in the public domain. Jeeves, the famous butler, also appeared in the story.

Throw in movies, spin-off books, and other media created through the ages around public domain characters and I worried that I could have been sued for something very little that I could never anticipate.

After reading this lawsuit (whether the estate succeeds or not), I am very glad I scrapped that novel, as a very kind and generous Mr. Holmes did make an appearance.

GROUP REGISTRATION

In June 2020, the United States Copyright Office promulgated a rule that allows writers to register up to 50 short works (100-17,500 words) published online in a single registration.

This is a pretty big deal for freelancers, bloggers, and journalists, who until now, had no easy way to register their content. It also has implications for self-published writers.

For example, if you publish short stories on your website (like a Ray Bradbury Challenge) or if you give short stories away every week on your blog like Kristine Kathryn Rusch does, you can now register those works, assuming they are text-only and published within a 90-day period. This does not apply to books; for most self-published writers, it applies to blogs.

I mostly had questions as I read the final rule from the Copyright Office.

My understanding is that a group registration will explicitly list each of the individual works directly. Is there a benefit to publishing your work online first (such as on your website) and then registering the work as a group? Would this give you potentially better and stronger copyright ownership than registering all of the stories under a single collection whose public registration record does not specify the individual works except in the sample you provide to the Copyright Office? Not sure if I know the answer.

Also, what about podcasts and video works? My YouTube channel has almost 300 videos. There's no way I'm registering each video separately. My podcast *The Writer's Journey* has 52 episodes per year, and my podcast *Writing Tip of the Day* has around 275 episodes per year. As is, I can't register them easily.

I can't help but wonder if we'll see group registrations introduced for podcasts and web content at some point.

WHAT MIGHT THE FALL OF INDIES LOOK LIKE?

I mentioned in the introduction of this book that one day the self-publishing sector will fall on hard times, much like traditional publishers are experiencing with the pandemic.

What will that look like?

What events would precipitate a decline in indie author income?

I don't know. Global economic recession or depression is my first thought.

A close second is a trend away from books toward more interactive experiences—gaming, movies, or even virtual reality in the long-term. Authors who don't pivot will be left behind.

Also, another event that might initiate this is Amazon taking some sort of action that hurts all authors, such as reducing its sales commissions, or restricting the 70% commission to KDP Select authors only, or introducing some sort of new sales commission scheme that drives authors to make less money overall. This happens all the time.

Another might be a traditional publisher "come back." Maybe the pandemic forces traditional publishers to figure out that they need to start innovating and spend a lot of money on technology and marketing value-adds for its authors, enticing more people to seek traditional publishing (and sign the same old terrible contracts). Perhaps innovation technology gives them a clear market advantage over indies, maybe through artificial intelligence. They'll undergo a brand refresh as well.

It's also not hard to imagine a political event that precipitates a societal distaste for self-publishing, such as a self-published writer who commits a mass murder and leaves behind a trail of books that espouse hatred and very obvious motives. I pray to God that never happens, as it would turn governments and public sentiment against indie writers.

But honestly, I don't know what an extinction event for indies would look like, or how bad it would be. It's worth asking the question, as when it happens, it will seem like it came out of nowhere, but will have been glaringly obvious in retrospect.

I think the sole reliance on the book as we know it is a liability. I also think not diversifying your books across all retailers is another warning sign. KDP Select is a game of musical chairs. You don't want to be playing the game when the music stops.

Other than that, I don't know, but it will be very, very interesting to see how resilient the indie community is through the decades.

HOW LONG WILL SMARTPHONES LAST?

Will the smartphone be with us forever?

While they have helped to improve our lives, there is growing evidence that they may be harmful to our health.

It's not implausible to imagine younger generations, perhaps those that haven't been born yet, seeking to abandon smartphones in favor of more experience-driven technology that is less obtrusive and allows them to interact with their environment. That technology could take many forms, many of which haven't been conceived yet, so it's not worth exploring them.

Might the smartphone be a "old folk thing" to our descendants? Will we reminisce what it was like to have iOS and Android devices much like we reminisce about rotary and flip phones today?

If the "handheld device" as we know it were removed from our lives, how would that change how we write, publish, and market? In other words, how does the device-less writer write and reach the device-less reader?

Audio and voice are the first technologies that come to mind along with augmented and virtual reality.

In the future, could people turn anything into a speaker or a screen? Will vibrations become a part of our nonverbal communication? Or will we avoid that altogether and control technology with our minds?

IDEAS YOU CAN STEAL

PLANNER FOR WRITERS

I've always thought that a dedicated physical planner for writers would be a great idea. I bought a Passion Planner last year and loved it. There's something pleasant about writing your goals down on pen and paper.

My hunch is that a planner that helped writers track their word counts, their book's progress, and maybe their emotional state in addition to the usual planner items would be well-received in our community. Especially if it was beautiful.

Planners are consistently a top product on Kickstarter. If the right author did it, they could get it funded, no problem.

CROWDFUNDING IN REVERSE

Kickstarter needs no introduction.

But what if there was a Kickstarter in reverse?

What if there was a site where customers could post problems they wish there was a solution to? What if entrepreneurs could review the problems, find ways to solve them, and then submit proposals with an explanation of what they can do, a completion date, and a dollar amount? The platform would facilitate an automated interview process where customers could ask questions and the entrepreneurs could revise their proposals if needed. Then the customers would pledge a dollar amount to fund the proposal they want to see turned into reality. If the project funds, the entrepreneur receives half the money upfront and the final half upon delivery of the project and an 80% or higher customer satisfaction rate.

It could be a discovery platform for entrepreneurs looking for problems to solve, and a win for customers who can articulate needs that entrepreneurs may not have thought of.

A platform like this would have tremendous benefits for writers. It could be a clever way for us to drive competition between writing apps, for example. If writing apps don't evolve to do what we want them to do, let's pay someone who will do the job. There would be unlimited potential.

GIVING YOUR BOOK AWAY ON
TORRENT SITES

A torrent site is a special type of peer-to-peer file-sharing protocol that takes a single file and breaks it into many pieces that your computer has to download. Your computer downloads those pieces from other downloaders' computers all over the world, and once it has all the pieces, it reassembles them together so that you can open the download. It is a highly sophisticated form of file sharing, and while it is legitimate, it is often used for illegal purposes, such as film or pornography downloads. Torrent sites such as "The Pirate Bay" are considered seedy underbellies of piracy.

What if you gave your books away on a torrent site? What would happen?

I have no idea because I've always chickened out at the idea. But I would think a genre like LitRPG could find a new audience on a torrent site. If you accept pirates as they are—a different but valid audience for your work—then interesting things could happen.

Torrent sites are not for the faint of heart, but maybe there's something there.

A BOOK COVER DESIGN YOUTUBE CHANNEL

Have you ever noticed how so many self-published authors choose to design their own book covers, yet there are almost no proven resources for them to learn the art of cover design?

Sure, you can learn design fundamentals, but that doesn't teach you how to design a book cover. Not specifically.

If I were a (good) book cover designer, here's what I would do.

I would start a YouTube channel teaching the ins and outs of book cover design. I'd show how I design my covers, letting people watch live as I designed a cover. I'd also teach the nuances of Photoshop, GIMP, or other design apps, and I'd teach authors design theory and how to make their book covers better. I'd teach how to design tasteful ads and other marketing materials for their books too. I'd write *the* definitive book on cover design and make *the* definitive premium course. That doesn't exist yet.

My content would make a real difference in authors' design skills, and therefore their sales.

I'd also expand the channel into book formatting since it's complementary. Heck, I might even find a formatter co-host who does separate videos on the channel but in the same style so we could build our volume and ad revenue quickly. We could team up a few times a year and do a *This Old House*-style segment where we take an author who has a horrendous cover and interior formatting, and revamp it free of charge as a way to market the channel and give back to the community.

The channel would be a resource for the industry, but most importantly, it would be the primary way I get clients. I'd have so many clients that I'd be booked months in advance.

As I said before, I'd have to be a good designer. Good designers are rare.

Design is a completely foreign world to authors. A book cover design channel on YouTube would be the only one of its kind, and therefore easy to stand out.

IP PATROLLER

I mentioned in the data section how it's a good idea to think about your books as real estate.

Landlords that have a lot of properties hire property managers. Property managers take care of the maintenance, screening for tenants, and any other issues that come up at a property.

Why not have *intellectual* property managers? Instead of a person, I believe this can best be accomplished with software.

Let's say that there's an app called Rover. Rover knows every intimate detail of your books because it connects to your book database. Rover patrols all of the retailers where you publish your books, looking for any problems. If Rover sees the wrong price, he alerts you via email. If the HTML in your book description breaks, he lets you know. He'll even check to verify that the right version of your book is for sale. If you *don't* hear from him, you'll know that everything with your books is fine.

Rover might even keep watch on the other books in your genre, and he could alert you when trends change and your book needs to adapt; he could let you know when it might be time to change your cover, for example. Rover could be a short and long-term tool.

Rover is what I call a yet-to-exist class of software called intellectual property management applications. These apps would treat your books as data and alert you on discrepancies. In a perfect world, they could fix the problems for you, but that's unlikely to happen.

Once, I did a book promo but forgot to change the price from $0.99 back to the original price. I didn't find out about the problem for six months. I lost a lot of money—four figures worth of income. Rover could have spotted that problem immediately and thus saved me money.

In talking about this concept on my channels, my experience is that most indie authors don't understand the need for this software yet, mainly because they don't have enough books for it to be a problem yet. But if our mantra as a community is that we want to make a career out of writing, that means a decent amount of authors will be prolific enough to have this problem long-term.

BOOK MARKETING BROWSER PLUGIN

We need our book metadata often. We may need to give readers a specific link to Barnes & Noble, or fill out a promo form with all our Book 1's basic details, or send our book information to a podcast host.

I envision a browser plugin that gives you easy access to all of your book metadata so that if you need it, you can select the book in the plugin, and the plugin will auto-populate most of the book's info for you. The plugin might also automatically take you to any folders on your computer for that specific book so you don't have to click around to find the right folders.

Think of it like a password wallet like LastPass, LogMeIn, or the Safari keychain, but for your books. Pick the book you want, and the plugin auto-populates as much data as it can. If desired, you could export data from the plugin too. You could also integrate the plugin into a database so that the database feeds the plugin.

Database idea aside, I don't believe this would be too difficult to program.

AUTHOR MARKETING CO-OP

I received a question from an author who asked if there were "self-publishing marketing co-ops." The author had experience with buying advertising through a local small business co-op and wondered if the indie community had the same thing.

A co-op is when multiple businesses pool their money to create a marketing outreach that is bigger than any of the businesses could achieve by themselves. For example, when I moved into my new house, I receive a generous book full of coupons from small businesses in the area—restaurants, insurance agents, contractors, garden centers, and more. Each business paid their fair share to produce the book. If you shop with one of the businesses, you're more likely to shop with another because they have referral programs.

While I don't think that there is a formal way to do this at the moment, I do think indies can pool their collective dollars for marketing. Authors do it for box sets and compilations all the time. It would be interesting to see authors find new ways to cross-promote each other using some kind of co-op. I think this could be particularly effective if all of the authors used direct sales. It would also be interesting if a book retailer tried this with authors in the same genre, using their platform to boost the sales of the authors, perhaps at an affordable rate for the authors to purchase the service.

MICROSOFT EXCEL FOR WRITERS

Microsoft Excel and (most) writers don't mix. However, there are many authors in the community who are masters at Excel. It would be great if one (or a few) of them wrote how-to books or created easy-to-consume courses to help the community get better at data analysis and get the most out of Excel.

There are books and courses out there, but I find that they are more complicated than most authors need. It's also hard to apply the concepts in general audience Excel videos to our situation as writers. It would be great to learn from someone who understands the community.

The simpler, the better. The goal should be to help authors feel more confident in Excel. If they can walk away with a basic framework of how to manipulate data, and maybe a few tips and tricks that they can use every day, I think an Excel book or course for writers could do well. At a minimum, it could recoup the cost of production.

PERSONALIZED EDITING RULES ENGINE

Before I share this idea, I acknowledge that it's not easy to reduce the English language into code. Our language has chewed up and spit out legions of programmers and data scientists trying to solve this problem.

That said, I do think there is more we can do.

In my line of work as an insurance consultant, one of my responsibilities is to review the company's business rules engine. The engine is an IBM product called ODM, which stands for Operational Decision Management, which is an engine that maintains a series of if-then rules that serve as the "brain" of the business's operations.

To use an oversimplified example, let's pretend I have an ice cream shop.

If a new customer purchases ice cream, then the system will print a 20% off coupon for their next purchase.

If an existing customer purchases ice cream in an amount greater than $10, they also get a 20% off coupon.

If an out-of-state customer makes a purchase, they receive a print-out with the ice cream shop's website and a call-to-action to share on social media. After all, it makes zero sense to give them a coupon if they're just passing through.

This means that existing customers who spend less than $10 and out-of-state customers don't receive a coupon. These rules would be programmed into the ice cream shop's point of sale system and could be tweaked at any time.

How could we apply this to the English language? As I said before, it would be foolish to try to create a rules engine for the entire English language. That's a fool's errand. But what if you could build an engine whose sole focus was to help you clean up your manuscript by identifying past mistakes your editor had to correct?

I envision the development of this app as a series of steps.

First, you would need some way to classify every word in the English language. You would need the app to distinguish between verbs, nouns, adverbs, prepositions, and so on. There are college linguistics departments that provide open-source libraries that contain this information—Princeton immediately comes to mind. Much of this work has already been done.

The app would also need to know tenses, conditions, as well as context. Take the word *ride*—it can be a noun or a verb depending on the context. This would be the trickiest part. A developer could start with the five hundred most common words in the English language and program those first to create a minimum viable product.

Next, once you have every word properly classified, then you could start programming rules. Let the author do it using an easy way to construct if-then statements, much like Apple iTunes allows you to create Smart Playlists.

The equation would be: **if-then statement + action.**

For example, let's say that my editor makes a change to my manuscript because I wrote the sentence "I want cookie sandwich." I left out the article "a" and the sentence should have said "I want a cookie sandwich."

The rule might read "If noun follows verb, look for [article] between them. If one does not exist, highlight the noun and the verb." The rule would run on every book moving forward to help me catch the same error.

Let's also say that my editor makes a change to my manuscript because I used the word *cadence* incorrectly in a sentence.

The rule might read "If word CADENCE is used, highlight every instance of the word."

Let's say that I have a bad habit of using the same word repetitively.

Take the paragraph "Eating ice cream is important. As a historical national treasure, its importance cannot be understated. It is also important to note that only 50 percent of dessert eaters prefer ice cream."

As you can tell, I used *important* way too much.

The rule might read "if ANY WORD other than [common articles, common prepositions] appears more than once within the same 250 word radius, highlight each instance of the word." I can then review each instance to verify if a change is needed. I could also tweak the radius if I wanted. A rule like this could easily be programmed to police your use of the word "I" in first-person stories, as another example.

I could also program rules that catch if I write numerals instead of spelling out numbers. Editors usually have standards on what you should do in a certain situation as dictated by the style manuals they adhere to; these rules could easily be programmed. For instance, if I write the word *forty* when I should use the numeral 40 instead, the rules can easily catch that.

Compared to mapping the entire English language, I think

this alternative could be slightly more doable. It would require you to understand how to form effective if-then statements. Perhaps artificial intelligence could help, but this technology may best be coded by a developer.

This could also be very effective if it could run in real-time while you were writing so that it could alert you to potential problems while you were typing.

If someone could pull this off, a personalized rule engine could be a game-changer for writers wanting to catch more errors in their manuscripts.

AUDIOBOOK TRANSITION TOOL

Writing with the audio version of your book in mind is not a skill that comes naturally to me.

When I recorded my first audiobook, I found several instances in my writing that did not translate well into audio. If I had known that before recording, I would have made changes.

It would be insightful to solicit feedback from a few dozen professional audiobook narrators to find out what irritates them when they're doing their readings.

Take the narrators' feedback, program as much of that feedback as you can into rules, and then create a simple app or Microsoft Word plugin that can scan an author's text and highlight words or sections that won't translate well into audio. You wouldn't be able to catch everything, but you would be able to capture some important items. The author can then make the necessary changes across their ebook, paperback, and audiobook script so that all versions of their book are consistent.

This tool could be integrated into the personalized rules engine I mentioned too.

Since audiobook is a permanent format, it pays to make sure

your book is as perfect as it can be before the narrator starts recording.

BRAND MONITORING SYSTEM

I've yet to find a brand monitoring system that works well.

Google Alerts works sometimes, but it's notoriously inconsistent.

A successful author needs a comprehensive brand monitoring system that alerts them whenever they or their books are mentioned on the Internet. Social media monitoring sites exist, but an author needs more than that. They need to know if an influencer reviews their book on their blog, or if someone mentions them on a podcast or YouTube channel. They also need to know as soon as possible in case they want to take some kind of action, such as sharing it with their audience. It's bad form to thank someone for shouting out your book six months after they mention it...better late than never, but it makes you look silly.

Also, understanding what people are saying about you in real-time helps you make better decisions about your business.

A COMPANY THAT MAINTAINS YOUR BOOKS WHEN YOU DIE

Every author will die, whether they like it or not.

When you die, who will maintain the rights to your books? Who will make sure they remain for sale? Who will update the book covers when they go stale? Who will answer the email when Hollywood wants to make a movie?

If you have a spouse or child who is willing to manage those rights, then that's the answer.

But many authors don't have spouses or children, or they don't have spouses or children who know how or want to manage their books. The result is that, if we do nothing, generations of authors will die, and their books will die with them. That's a shame because books generate income whether we're alive or not, and that's money our families can use.

Imagine a company that says "Sign a contract with us. When you die, we'll take the rights to your books and we'll keep them for sale so that readers can always buy them. We'll take a commission and pass the remaining royalties to your family each month. If you pay us an additional fee, we'll even change your covers and book descriptions as trends change for the next ten years. While you're alive, you keep your rights and we have no interest in your work. When you die, we'll be there for your family."

Basically, it would be a traditional publisher, but for when you die. The product would function like an annuity, but for your beneficiaries.

When you consider that more people will continue to trend toward indie publishing, you have a renewable audience every year.

I'm making this sound simple, but building a company like this would be far from simple. For starters, you'd be in court a lot. The legal fees would be extraordinary. You'd need a solid way of eliminating fraud and the handling of illegitimate children that pop up out of nowhere.

But the right person could start this company and turn it into a unicorn. The company could effortlessly expand into music and the arts. With enough leverage, you could offer a marketplace to Hollywood and other subsidiary rights buyers who can purchase rights cheaply, easily, and without fear of contractual lawsuits, assuming the company could properly vet authors and their estate situations. Beneficiaries would get pleasant emails whenever a right has been purchased, and a nice payday in their bank account along with a copy of the agreement.

The platform could also automate and simplify intellectual property agreements so that no humans ever talk to each other. The company would have all the leverage because it would control the terms at which rights buyers come to the table.

To put the potential vise-grip this company could have on the marketplace into perspective, consider the company Upwork, the freelancer platform. Upwork provides access to talented freelancers, but places a number of controversial restrictions on its users. If users don't like it, then they can leave, but Upwork is the biggest game in town, so they don't want to leave.

Unlike a traditional publisher, who will only promote their top-selling titles, this company could explore artificial intelligence as a way for it to find ways to sell more of *everything* in its catalogue, possibly using AI and machine learning for pay-per-click advertising as I mentioned before. If the AI can purchase ads for even the most obscure books with confidence, with just a minimal return on investment, it would make the company wildly profitable.

All of this could work because authors all over the world have a dream: to get their books published. Many of them want their books to survive them.

CONTENT CREATED WHILE WRITING THIS BOOK

150 Self-Publishing Questions Answered (Book)

This book was written in a partnership between Michael and The Alliance of Independent Authors (ALLi, a nonprofit organization for self-published writers), and it answers the most common self-publishing questions in a conversational question and answer format. The audiobook is narrated by Michael!

Buy your copy at www.authorlevelup.com/150

Writing in Hard Times (Course)

Learn how to future-proof your writing business by learning the basics of risk management for writers. This course draws on Michael's experience in insurance protecting thousands of businesses every day. You'll learn how to protect your business, family, and your data from anything life throws your way. Never get caught off-guard again. As is typical with Michael, this is the only course of its kind in the writing community.

Enroll today at www.authorlevelup.com/hardtimes

. . .

Author Level Up YouTube Channel - Highlights

Watch at youtube.com/authorlevelup.

How Long Should Your Novel Be?

How much does it cost to publish a book?

Beta Readers: The ONLY Video You Will Ever Need

Read Like a Writer

Interviews & Appearances

The Sample Chapter Podcast: Michael discusses his fiction writing process, writer's block, and reads a chapter from his book, *Shadow Deal.*

Inspirational Indie Author Interviews with Howard Lovy: Michael appears in a montage of interviews with thoughts on how to write during lockdown and how to cope with the pandemic.

READ THE NEXT VOLUME

Michael's writer journey continues in the next volume of this series!

Grab your copy at www.authorlevelup.com/confidential.

MEET M.L. RONN

Science fiction and fantasy on the wild side!

M.L. Ronn (Michael La Ronn) is the author of many science fiction and fantasy novels including *The Good Necromancer*, *Android X,* and *The Last Dragon Lord* series.

In 2012, a life-threatening illness made him realize that storytelling was his #1 passion. He's devoted his life to writing ever since, making up whatever story makes him fall out of his chair laughing the hardest. Every day.

Learn more about Michael
www.authorlevelup.com (for writers)
www.michaellaronn.com (fiction)

MORE BOOKS BY M.L. RONN

Books for Writers:

www.authorlevelup.com/books

Fiction:
www.michaellaronn.com/books